W9-AQY-777

It's My State!

TEXAS

The Lone Star State

Linda Jacobs Altman, Tea Benduhn, and Hex Kleinmartin

Cavendish Square

New York

Published in 2015 by Cavendish Square Publishing, LLC
243 5th Avenue, Suite 136, New York, NY 10016

Copyright © 2015 by Cavendish Square Publishing, LLC

First Edition

No part of this publication may be reproduced, stored in a retrieval system, or transmitted in any form or by any means—electronic, mechanical, photocopying, recording, or otherwise—without the prior permission of the copyright owner. Request for permission should be addressed to Permissions, Cavendish Square Publishing, 243 5th Avenue, Suite 136, New York, NY 10016. Tel (877) 980-4450; fax (877) 980-4454.

Website: cavendishsq.com

This publication represents the opinions and views of the author based on his or her personal experience, knowledge, and research. The information in this book serves as a general guide only. The author and publisher have used their best efforts in preparing this book and disclaim liability rising directly or indirectly from the use and application of this book.

CPSIA Compliance Information: Batch #WW15CSQ

All websites were available and accurate when this book was sent to press.

Library of Congress Cataloging-in-Publication Data

Kleinmartin, Hex.
Texas / Hex Kleinmartin, Linda Jacobs Altman and Tea Benduhn.
pages cm. — (It's my state!)
Includes index.
ISBN 978-1-50260-017-2 (hardcover) ISBN 978-1-50260-018-9 (ebook)
1. Texas—Juvenile literature. I. Altman, Linda Jacobs, 1943- II. Benduhn, Tea. III. Title.

F386.3.K54 2015
976.4—dc23

2014026352

Editor: Fletcher Doyle
Senior Copy Editor: Wendy A. Reynolds
Art Director: Jeffrey Talbot
Designer: Joseph Macri
Senior Production Manager: Jennifer Ryder-Talbot
Production Editor: David McNamara
Photo Research by J8 Media

The photographs in this book are used by permission and through the courtesy of: Cover photo by Tim Fitzharris/Minden Pictures/Getty Images; rheisch/iStock/Thinkstock, 4; chris froome/Shutterstock.com, 4; Getty Images: Robert Frerck, 4; IMNATURE/iStock/Thinkstock, 5; Dennis Lane Photography, 5 (center); Harald Sund (bottom), 5; Joel Sartore/National Geographic/Getty Images, 6; Shutterstock: Mike Norton, 8; Alamy: © offiwent.com, 9; © Joe Baraban, 14; © Danita Delimont, 15; Tphotography/Shutterstock.com, 16; Jeremy Woodhouse, 16; Daderot/File:Dinosaur exhibit - Houston Museum of Natural Science - DSC01881.JPG/Wikimedia Commons, 17; Witold Skrypczak/Lonely Planet Images/Getty Images, 17; Billy Hathorn/File:Cattle sculpture outside National Ranching Heritage Center IMG 0243.JPG/Wikimedia Commons, 17; Gary Yim, 19; James Hager/Robert Harding World Imagery/Getty Images, 20; Matt Jeppson/Shutterstock.com, 20; SambaPhoto/Araquem Alcantara (top), 20; Steve Maslowski (center), 21; Donovan Reese(bottom), 21; Harald Sund, 21; © Visions of America, LLC, 22; SuperStock, 24; Library of Congress: Historic American Buildings Survey, 25; Bridgeman Art Library/Getty Images, 27; Courtesy State Preservation Board; Austin; TX; Original Artist: Huddle; William H. 1847–1892; Photographer: unknown; Pre 1991. Pre Conservation./© State Preservation Board (2010), Austin, Texas. All rights reserved, including further reproduction, commercial display, incorporation into other works, or conversion to digital media, 29; Dvortygirl/File:Yarndoll9.jpg/Wikimedia Commons, 30; TabooTikiGod/ File:Remember Your Regiment, U.S. Army in Action Series, 2d Dragoons charge in Mexican War 1846.jpg/Wikimedia Commons, 33; Jorg Hackemann/Shutterstock.com, 34; Murat Taner/Photographer's Choice/Getty Images, 34; Adam Jones, 34; Action Sports Photography/Shutterstock.com, 35; Simiprof at English Wikipedia/File:TAMUCC island.jpg/Wikimedia Commons, 35; Ricardo Garza/Shutterstock.com, 35; © North Wind Picture Archives, 37; NASA, 39; Joseph Scherschel/Time & Life Pictures, 40; © Steve Hamblin, 44; Gib Martinez, 46; © Jeff Greenberg, 47; AFP/Getty Images, 48; Brad Barket/Getty Images, 48; JOE KLAMAR/AFP/Getty Images, 48; Hulton Archive/Getty Images, 49; Andrew H. Walker/Getty Images, 49; Michael Tran/FilmMagic (center), 49; © offiwent.com, 51; © Michael Diggin, 52; John Moore/Getty Images, 53; Ed Schipul/File:JigGirlsGalveston2006.jpg/Wikimedia Commons, 54; Bloomberg/Getty Images, 54; AP Photo/The Shawnee News Star, Jennifer Pitts, 55; Phillip Holland, 55; J Raedle, 56; J Raedle, 58; Nevin Reid, 59; AP Images: Harry Cabluck, 60; Arnold Newman/File:Lyndon B. Johnson, photo portrait, leaning on chair, color.jpg/Wikimedia Commons, 62; Harris & Ewing, Inc./File:Sam Rayburn.jpg/Wikimedia Commons, 62; Shelly Katz, 62; State Preservation Board, Austin, TX: Surrender of Santa Anna 1989. 62; Walter Bibikow, 64; Rick Gershon, 66; Hulton Archive/Getty Images, 67; NASA/Bill Stafford/File:STS-135 Rex Walheim and Sandy Magnus in the Neutral Buoyancy Laboratory.jpg/Wikimedia Commons, 68; Joe Raedle, 68; silver-joh, 68; David / File:South Padre Sunrise 1.jpg/Wikimedia Commons, 69; Skip Brown/National Geographic/Getty Images, 69; Mark Green, 69; Jupiterimages/Stockbyte/Thinkstock, 70; Frank Whitney, 71; Mark S. Wexler, 72; Mike Carlo/File:Cyanocorax luxuosus Laguna Atascosa NWR Texas.jpg/Wikimedia Commons, 75; Leaflet/ File:Brazos Double Mtn Fork 2009.jpg/Wikimedia Commons, 75.

Printed in the United States of America

TEXAS
CONTENTS

A QUICK LOOK AT
STATEHOOD: DECEMBER 29, 1845

State Plant: Prickly Pear Cactus

The prickly pear, the most common cactus in Texas, has flat pads that hold water. A staple in many Texas kitchens, its fruit can be peeled and tossed into salads or served alone as a vegetable. It also makes a delicious jelly.

State Flower: Bluebonnet

Bluebonnets grow in uncultivated pastures and also along highways, where they were planted by the Texas Department of Transportation. The bluebonnet has its own song, festival, and town: Ennis, the Bluebonnet City of Texas.

State Bird: Mockingbird

Mockingbirds are natural mimics—they can imitate the songs and sounds of other birds. They are also uncommonly brave. Nesting mockingbirds have been known to swoop down on dogs, cats, and even people who "invade" their territory.

TEXAS

POPULATION: 25,145,561

★ State Tree: Pecan

The pecan became the official state tree in 1919 in honor of James Stephen Hogg, the first native-born governor of Texas. When Hogg died in 1906, he left an unusual last request—he wanted a pecan tree planted on his grave.

★ State Dish: Chili

No dish says "Texas" better than a steaming hot bowl of chili. The state's Chili Appreciation Society hosts an annual world championship chili cook-off in the town of Terlingua. Cooks from around the state come to compete with their best recipes.

★ State Folk Dance: Square Dance

This lively dance features a "square" of couples performing patterned steps. A caller sings out steps, such as "allemande," "sashay," and "promenade," in time to the music. Square dance clubs all over the state offer classes for beginners and hold competitions for experienced dancers.

Texas is home to over 11 million cattle that graze on the state's expansive prairies and ranches.

The Lone Star State

Texas is the second-largest state in the nation, after Alaska. It covers about 261,797 square miles (691,027 square kilometers) of the south-central United States. Within this vast territory are many landforms, including the beaches and marshlands of the Gulf **Coast** and the sagebrush and cacti of the southwestern desert. In between are hills and canyons, wide grassland prairies, and forests thick with trees.

Texas is made up of 254 counties—by far the most of any state. Austin, the state capital, is in Travis County. The biggest city, Houston, is in Harris County. Texas is usually divided into four geographic areas: the arid mountains and basins region in the far west, the Great Plains in the northwest and north-central part of the state, the central lowlands in the middle, and the Gulf Coastal Plain in the east and southeast. These main areas are in turn divided into sub-regions.

West Texas

The mountains and basins region is also called Big Bend country. A large loop, or bend, in the Rio Grande ("big river" in Spanish) forms the southern border and separates Texas from Mexico. Stretching from Midland-Odessa in the northeast to Del Rio in the southeast, Big Bend country covers 41,000 square miles (106,190 sq. km).

Big Bend country is a place of windblown basins, or lowlands, and craggy mountain ranges. The area includes the Guadalupe Range, the only true mountains in Texas. The range is home to Guadalupe Peak; at 8,749 feet (2,667 meters), it is the state's tallest peak. The area is also home to Big Bend National Park and Guadalupe Mountains National Park.

Distances in Big Bend country are vast, and water is in short supply. The area averages only 12 inches (30 centimeters) of rainfall a year. Mostly because of the lack of water, Big Bend country has very few people. Its only large city is El Paso, which had a population of around 650,000 in 2010.

About 265 million years ago, during the Permian era, the arid landscape of Guadalupe Mountains National Park was actually covered by a vast tropical sea.

The Glass Mountains in West Texas are famous for the many Permian-era fossils found there.

The high plains region of the Texas Panhandle lies to the northeast of Big Bend country. This dry plateau (raised flat land) is split in the north by the Canadian River. The weather can vary wildly. Stiff winds sweep across the prairie, raising clouds of sand. Sudden downpours turn dry riverbeds into channels for flash floods. Storms called "blue northers" bring freezing winds from the Rocky Mountains.

The Panhandle is cattle country. Herds of beef cattle graze the short, tough buffalo grass that covers the prairie. Though the region is roughly the size of West Virginia, its total population is only about 500,000. About 410,000 of those residents live in the two biggest cities, Amarillo and Lubbock. The rest are spread among ranches and country towns so small that they do not even have a grocery store.

Central Texas

The Caprock Escarpment is a steep cliff on the eastern edge of the Panhandle plateau. It separates the high plains of the Panhandle from the lower central plains. The northern part of this region is often called the rolling plains because of its gentle hills. Like the Panhandle, it is part of the Great Plains of the American Midwest. This vast area was once a tallgrass prairie that supported huge herds of bison. Today, the bison are gone and so is the tall grass, and the region is the most populated in Texas, with most people clustered in the Dallas-Fort Worth area.

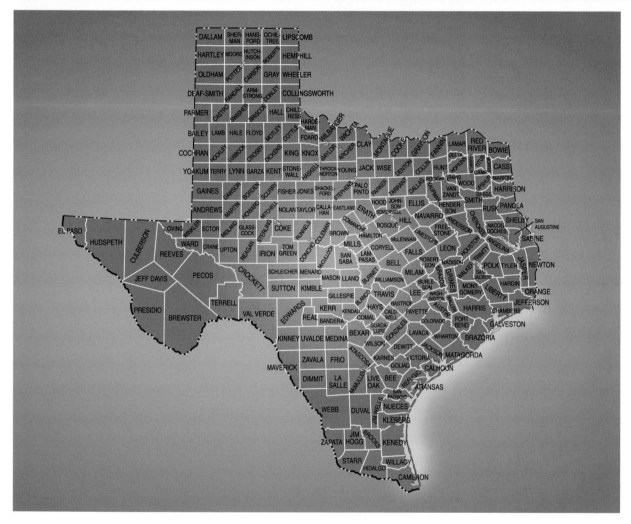

Anderson County	58,458	Bailey County	7,165	Borden County	641
Andrews County	14,786	Bandera County	20,485	Bosque County	18,212
Angelina County	86,771	Bastrop County	74,171	Bowie County	92,565
Aransas County	23,158	Baylor County	3,726	Brazoria County	313,166
Archer County	9,054	Bee County	31,861	Brazos County	194,851
Armstrong County	1,901	Bell County	310,235	Brewster County	9,232
Atascosa County	44,911	Bexar County	1,714,773	Briscoe County	1,637
Austin County	28,417	Blanco County	10,497	Brooks County	7,223

TEXAS

County	Population	County	Population	County	Population
Brown County	38,106	Crane County	4,375	Fort Bend County	585,375
Burleson County	17,187	Crockett County	3,719	Franklin County	10,605
Burnet County	42,750	Crosby County	6,059	Freestone County	19,816
Caldwell County	38,066	Culberson County	2,398	Frio County	17,217
Calhoun County	21,381	Dallam County	6,703	Gaines County	17,526
Callahan County	13,544	Dallas County	2,368,139	Galveston County	291,309
Cameron County	406,220	Dawson County	13,833	Garza County	6,461
Camp County	12,401	Deaf Smith County	19,372	Gillespie County	24,837
Carson County	6,182	Delta County	5,231	Glasscock County	1,226
Cass County	30,464	Denton County	662,614	Goliad County	7,210
Castro County	8,062	DeWitt County	20,097	Gonzales County	19,807
Chambers County	35,096	Dickens County	2,444	Gray County	22,535
Cherokee County	50,845	Dimmit County	9,996	Grayson County	120,877
Childress County	7,041	Donley County	3,677	Gregg County	121,730
Clay County	10,752	Duval County	11,782	Grimes County	26,604
Cochran County	3,127	Eastland County	18,583	Guadalupe County	131,533
Coke County	3,320	Ector County	137,130	Hale County	36,273
Coleman County	8,895	Edwards County	2,002	Hall County	3,353
Collin County	782,341	Ellis County	149,610	Hamilton County	8,517
Collingsworth County	3,057	El Paso County	800,647	Hansford County	5,613
Colorado County	20,874	Erath County	37,890	Hardeman County	4,139
Comal County	108,472	Falls County	17,866	Hardin County	54,635
Comanche County	13,974	Fannin County	33,915	Harris County	4,092,459
Concho County	4,087	Fayette County	24,554	Harrison County	65,631
Cooke County	38,437	Fisher County	3,974	Hartley County	6,062
Coryell County	75,388	Floyd County	6,446	Haskell County	5,899
Cottle County	1,505	Foard County	1,336	Hays County	157,107

County	Population	County	Population	County	Population
Hemphill County	3,807	Kerr County	49,625	Mason County	4,012
Henderson County	78,532	Kimble County	4,607	Matagorda County	36,702
Hidalgo County	774,769	King County	286	Maverick County	54,258
Hill County	35,089	Kinney County	3,598	Medina County	46,006
Hockley County	22,935	Kleberg County	32,061	Menard County	2,242
Hood County	51,182	Knox County	3,719	Midland County	136,872
Hopkins County	35,161	Lamar County	49,793	Milam County	24,757
Houston County	23,732	Lamb County	13,977	Mills County	4,936
Howard County	35,012	Lampasas County	19,677	Mitchell County	9,403
Hudspeth County	3,476	La Salle County	6,886	Montague County	19,719
Hunt County	86,129	Lavaca County	19,263	Montgomery County	455,746
Hutchinson County	22,150	Lee County	16,612	Moore County	21,904
Irion County	1,599	Leon County	16,801	Morris County	12,934
Jack County	9,044	Liberty County	75,643	Motley County	1,210
Jackson County	14,075	Limestone County	23,384	Nacogdoches County	64,524
Jasper County	35,710	Lipscomb County	3,302	Navarro County	47,735
Jeff Davis County	2,342	Live Oak County	11,531	Newton County	14,445
Jefferson County	252,273	Llano County	19,301	Nolan County	15,216
Jim Hogg County	5,300	Loving County	82	Nueces County	340,223
Jim Wells County	40,838	Lubbock County	278,831	Ochiltree County	10,223
Johnson County	150,934	Lynn County	5,915	Oldham County	2,052
Jones County	20,202	McCulloch County	8,283	Orange County	81,837
Karnes County	14,824	McLennan County	234,906	Palo Pinto County	28,111
Kaufman County	103,350	McMullen County	707	Panola County	23,796
Kendall County	33,410	Madison County	13,664	Parker County	116,927
Kenedy County	416	Marion County	10,546	Parmer County	10,269
Kent County	808	Martin County	4,799	Pecos County	15,507

TEXAS
POPULATION BY COUNTY

County	Population	County	Population	County	Population
Polk County	45,413	Starr County	60,968	Wharton County	41,280
Potter County	121,073	Stephens County	9,630	Wheeler County	5,410
Presidio County	7,818	Sterling County	1,143	Wichita County	131,500
Rains County	10,914	Stonewall County	1,490	Wilbarger County	13,535
Randall County	120,725	Sutton County	4,128	Willacy County	22,134
Reagan County	3,367	Swisher County	7,854	Williamson County	422,679
Real County	3,309	Tarrant County	1,809,034	Wilson County	42,918
Red River County	12,860	Taylor County	131,506	Winkler County	7,110
Reeves County	13,783	Terrell County	984	Wise County	59,127
Refugio County	7,383	Terry County	12,651	Wood County	41,964
Roberts County	929	Throckmorton County	1,641	Yoakum County	7,879
Robertson County	16,622	Titus County	32,334	Young County	18,550
Rockwall County	78,337	Tom Green County	110,224	Zapata County	14,018
Runnels County	10,501	Travis County	1,024,266	Zavala County	11,677
Rusk County	53,330	Trinity County	14,585		
Sabine County	10,834	Tyler County	21,766		
San Augustine County	8,865	Upshur County	39,309		
San Jacinto County	26,384	Upton County	3,355		
San Patricio County	64,804	Uvalde County	26,405		
San Saba County	6,131	Val Verde County	48,879		
Schleicher County	3,461	Van Zandt County	52,579		
Scurry County	16,921	Victoria County	86,793		
Shackelford County	3,378	Walker County	67,861		
Shelby County	25,448	Waller County	43,205		
Sherman County	3,034	Ward County	10,658		
Smith County	209,714	Washington County	33,718		
Somervell County	8,490	Webb County	250,304		

Source: U.S. Bureau of the Census, 2010

South of the rolling plains is the Edwards plateau, or hill country. The terrain is rugged, but not particularly high, as the maximum elevation is only 3,000 feet (914 m). The area, which is dotted with rivers, streams, and lakes, is known for its beauty and is considered the heart of Texas.

One of the most dramatic sub-regions in the state, the Balcones Canyonlands, lies northwest of Austin. It has cliff faces so steep they seem like walls, and exposed rock formations that were ancient long before human beings came to Texas.

East Texas

The coastal plain of East Texas is the largest natural region in the state. The northwestern part of the area is heavily forested with oak trees and other hardwoods. These forests alternate with blackland prairies, where the soil is dark and rich. Local Texans call this soil black "gumbo" after the thick, stew, like dish that is a Texas favorite.

To the east, along the Louisiana border, oaks and other hardwoods give way to pine trees. The piney woods, as the area is known, is part of a vast and ancient pine forest that once covered much of the southeast. At that time, the forest was dense, dark, and undisturbed. Even today, few people live in the piney woods. There are more farms, ranches, and lumber operations than cities and suburbs. The largest city in the region is Tyler, with more than ninety thousand people.

South of the piney woods, the Texas coastline follows the Gulf of Mexico. The Gulf Coast is a place of sandy beaches and wetlands, or marshes, teeming with wildlife, including whooping cranes and sea turtles.

East Texas is densely forested. Here, a forest worker checks the health of trees.

Inland from the gulf is the Rio Grande Valley—the southernmost tip of the coastal plain. The valley is a lowland desert, with mesquite trees, prickly pear cactus, and rootless tumbleweeds scurrying ahead of the wind. Irrigation systems (human-made watering systems) help make the valley's soil fertile. Farms there produce a variety of fruits and vegetables, including spinach, peanuts, and strawberries.

Texas has seventeen barrier islands that extend along the Gulf Coast. These landforms include Galveston Island (which contains the city of Galveston) and Padre Island. At 70 miles (113 km) long, Padre Island is the longest undeveloped stretch of barrier island in the world. As the name suggests, a barrier island is an offshore island that protects the mainland from high seas and storms. The Texas Gulf Coast is frequently hit by hurricanes and other tropical storms.

Climate

Joking about the **climate** is a Texas tradition. Texans have been known to say that their state has four seasons: drought, flood, blizzard, and twister (tornado). Like many jokes, this one has a grain of truth. All of these extremes can and do happen in Texas.

West Texas is the coldest part of the state, with an average annual temperature of 54 degrees Fahrenheit (12 degrees Celsius). Summer days are fiercely hot, but temperatures plunge at night. Even in July and August, west Texans often need a sweater after sunset. Winter brings blizzards that blanket the prairie in snow.

Few people think of snow when they think of Texas, but winters in some parts of the state can be harsh.

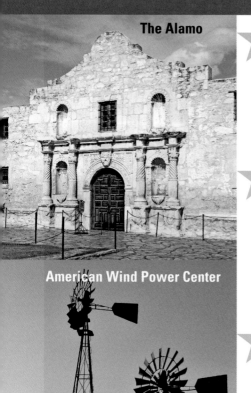

The Alamo

American Wind Power Center

Big Bend National Park

1. Alamo

This former Mission church and military garrison is the Shrine of Texas Liberty. It is most famous for the ninety-minute battle in 1836 between Mexican and Texan troops during the Texas Revolution. It is a short distance from San Antonio's River Walk.

2. American Wind Power Center

The invention of the self-governing windmill influenced the development of the western two-thirds of the United States. Tens of thousands were built between 1854 and 1920. This collection in Lubbock houses windmills, pumps, numerous photographs, and models.

3. Big Bend National Park

This spot in southwest Texas near Marathon is home to twenty-two species of bats, more than any other national park. There are more than 150 miles (241.5 km) of hiking trails, and dinosaur fossils from the last 35 million years of their existence have been found here.

4. Cascade Caverns

Complete with a 100-foot (30.5 meters) waterfall, many find these caverns in Boerne to be a great way to escape the sun and heat. **Native Americans** and hermits have lived in it, and mastodon tusks have been excavated from the cave as well.

5. Dealey Plaza

This is the site of the assassination of President John F. Kennedy in 1963. There is a two-story museum atop the Texas School Book Depository. It is believed the shot that killed the president was fired from there.

TEXAS ★ ★ ★ ★ ★ ★

6. The Houston Museum of Natural Science

This museum has exhibits of dinosaur fossils, gemstones, artifacts from ancient Egypt and the Americas, and wildlife from Africa and Texas. It also has the decommissioned battleship Texas, which is the first battleship memorial museum in the U.S.

7. Lone Star Flight Museum

Recognized by the State of Texas as the Texas Aviation Hall of Fame, the Galveston museum places special educational significance on the technological evolution of American aviation and its impact on aviation and world events.

8. National Border Patrol Museum

The Border Patrol has been in existence since 1924. Border Patrol vehicles on exhibit in this El Paso museum include an airplane, an ATV, a snowmobile, and a jeep and helicopter that museum visitors can sit in.

9. The National Ranching Heritage Center

This museum and historical park is located on the campus of Texas Tech University in Lubbock. There are exhibits on the history of ranching, as well as the culture, clothing, and artifacts of the cowboys who watched over the cattle.

10. State Capitol

The Texas Capitol in Austin is one of the nation's most distinguished state capitols. It was placed on the National Register of Historic Places in 1970 and designated a National Historic Landmark in 1986 for its "significant contribution to American history."

Houston Museum of Natural Science

Lone Star Flight Museum

National Ranching Heritage Center

The hottest part of Texas is the Rio Grande Valley, known for mild winters and crackling hot summers. The Gulf Coast escapes the hot summers because of the marine, or ocean, air from the Gulf of Mexico, but the humidity is high. Winters are equally mild, with no trace of snow. But this mild weather can be spoiled by fierce, often deadly storms coming from the gulf.

Wildlife

Like the climate and the land, Texas wildlife varies by region. It ranges from rattlesnakes and roadrunners in the western desert to beavers, raccoons, and white-tailed deer in the eastern woodlands.

Majestic whooping cranes winter on the Gulf Coast, and sea turtles swim just offshore. Alligators prowl the marshlands, occasionally coming into contact with human beings. Game wardens at the Texas Parks and Wildlife Department get fifty to sixty frantic "alligator calls" a year. In most cases, the caller has run over an alligator on the highway or found one in his or her backyard. When possible, game wardens trap the animals and release them into a wildlife preserve.

Kemp's Ridleys are the smallest and most endangered sea turtles in the world. They have an average length of 23 to 27.5 inches (58.5 to 70 cm) and average weight of 100 pounds (45 kg). The turtles' nesting areas are found only in Mexico and Texas. In the 1980s, these turtles were nearly extinct, but people in Mexico and Texas worked together and protected the turtle eggs in their nests. One of the efforts is named the Kemp's Ridley Sea Turtle Recovery Project and it is conducted on Texas' Padre Island National Seashore. Biologists watch for a nesting female to emerge on the beach—males live only in the water after they hatch—and then they take the eggs to an incubator for protected care. If biologists can't find the nest, they sometimes bring in a nest detector dog to help them find it. The dog, a Cairn Terrier named Ridley Ranger, found its first nest in 2006. After the eggs hatched, many of the babies were "head-started." This means that hatchlings were grown in captivity. When the turtles were big enough volunteers released them into the gulf.

There were only 702 nests for these turtles worldwide in 1985, the lowest total ever. However, there were about 21,797 nests found worldwide during 2012.

State of Brewster

Brewster County measures 6,193 square miles [16,039 sq. km] and is the largest county in Texas. It is larger than Connecticut and three times larger than Delaware.

The coatimundi is a social and noisy critter. It lives in groups of up to twenty-four animals, who spend much of their time chattering to each other.

The Rio Grande Valley has some of the state's most unusual animal species. Tropical creatures such as the ocelot and the coatimundi have migrated north from Mexico. The coatimundi, or coati for short, is related to the raccoon. It looks a bit like a raccoon, but has a longer face and tail. It looks for food in trees as well as on the ground, living mainly on insects.

The ocelot is a cat about twice the size of an ordinary house cat. It lives in the brush country of southern Texas, hunting birds, rabbits, and small rodents. The most striking feature of the ocelot is its beautiful spotted fur. For many years, its fur made the cat a favorite target for hunters. The ocelot has also suffered a loss of its habitat as dense brush was cleared for farmland. Today, the ocelot is on the U.S. government's endangered species list. Residents of the southern Rio Grande Valley are working to save this beautiful cat. They are restoring its habitat by planting native shrubs in some areas, and—as with any endangered animal—the hunting of ocelots has been outlawed.

Even in these days of disappearing wildlife habitats and fast-growing cities, Texas is still known for its wide open spaces. Modern Texans like things that way. They may be more likely to drive the highways than ride horses on the range, but they still treasure the land as an important part of their heritage.

Armadillo

Bat

Horned Lizard

1. Armadillo

No animal is more closely associated with Texas than the armadillo. This little roly-poly creature is about the size of a house cat and has a bony, scaly shell on its back to protect it from predators.

2. Bat

Bats are mammals whose forelimbs form webbed wings, making them the only mammals naturally capable of true and sustained flight. Thirty-two species of these winged mammals have been found in Texas, more than in any other state in the United States.

3. Cactus

Many kinds of cacti can be found in the deserts of Texas. Their thick fleshy stems act as a water-storage system. People lost without water can cut off a piece of some types of cacti and suck moisture from the pulp.

4. Cypress

Many of the species of cypress trees are adapted to forest fires, holding their seeds for many years in closed cones until the parent trees are killed by a fire. The seeds are then released to colonize the bare, burnt ground.

5. Horned Lizard

Horned lizards were once so abundant that the legislature made them the state reptile. Today, they are rare, but a group called the Texas Horned Lizard Conservation Society is working to protect the lizards and their habitat.

TEXAS

6. Javelina

Found in brushy semi desert where prickly pear, a favorite food, is found, the javelina was hunted **commercially** for its hide until 1939. They are harmless to livestock and to people, though they can defend themselves ferociously when attacked by hunting dogs.

7. Mesquite

Mesquite has crooked limbs that grow close to the ground, giving it a bushy appearance. It can grow tall enough to be called a tree, however. Mesquite is able to survive in dry climates thanks to a large and deep root system that makes good use of available water.

8. Pecan

The pecan is a species of hickory tree, whose name is from an Algonquian word, meaning a nut requiring a stone to crack. The wood is used in making furniture and wood flooring, as well as flavoring fuel for smoking meats.

9. Roadrunner

This long-tailed bird made famous by a cartoon can often be seen racing across the sands of West Texas. The roadrunner has two calls, a "co-coo-coo-coo-cooooo" and a clattering "whirr." Unlike the cartoon version, the real bird does not go "beep beep."

10. Wildflowers

Texas has about four thousand species of wildflowers. From the dainty bluebonnet to the majestic sunflower, the flowers grow in many colors and shapes.

Pecans

Roadrunner

Wildflowers

More than seven thousand years ago, prehistoric people created rock art called pictographs, such as these paintings found at Seminole Canyon State Park.

From the Beginning

Texas has been part of six different countries: It has flown the flags of Spain, France, Mexico, the Texas Republic, the United States, and—during the Civil War—the Confederacy. Texas's written history begins with the Spanish explorers of the sixteenth century. Its unwritten history goes back much further.

Long before European explorers arrived, Native Americans lived in all parts of what is now Texas. The early peoples included the Caddos in East Texas; the Atakapas and Karankawas along the coast; and the Tonkawas, Tiguas, and Kickapoos in the west.

First Flag: Spain, 1519-1821

Spanish interest in Texas began as early as 1519, when a sea captain named Alonzo Álvarez de Piñeda mapped the gulf coastline. The next explorers had heard legends of golden cities containing fabulous wealth for the taking. When they arrived, they found only an untamed and beautiful land occupied by people who cared nothing for gold.

In 1682, the first permanent European settlement was established near present-day El Paso. As the Spanish claimed and settled lands, they came into conflict with the people who already lived there. The European idea that individuals could own land was strange to the Native Americans. They knew nothing of deeds, land grants, and property rights. They believed that land belonged to no one; therefore, it belonged to everyone. But the Europeans kept coming. As a result, the Native Americans lost their land and their way of life.

Some tribes were conquered, and after members converted to Christianity, were made to work for the Spanish missions. The missions were not just churches. They were complete settlements. The main complex was usually walled in. Inside were workshops, supply rooms, and living quarters, as well as the church. Planted fields and pastureland surrounded the mission. The Native American converts lived at the mission and worked long, hard hours in the fields. They did not get paid for this work, nor were they allowed to leave.

Many of the indigenous people fell victim to European diseases such as smallpox and measles. Native peoples had no experience with these illnesses, and therefore no resistance, or immunity, to them. Entire tribes were wiped out by diseases.

The tribes that escaped this fate lived by raiding Spanish settlements. For as long as the Spanish flag flew over Texas, **settlers** were locked in an often-bloody struggle with the indigenous people they were trying to displace.

Second Flag: France, 1685-1763

When Europeans introduced horses to the Americas, the lives of Native Americans changed forever. Before they acquired horses, tribes such as the Apache used to follow and hunt buffalo on foot.

After the arrival of Europeans in Texas, many Native Americans were forced to live and work in Spanish missions such as Ysleta Mission in El Paso.

In 1685, King Louis XIV of France gave the explorer René-Robert Cavelier, sieur de La Salle, four ships and a royal command: La Salle was to set up a fort at the mouth of the Mississippi River in what is now Louisiana. Because of a navigational error, La Salle landed in East Texas rather than southern Louisiana, which he had explored several years earlier.

La Salle decided to make the best of the situation and built the fort in Texas. The result was Fort St. Louis, named in honor of the king. It was a group of seven log cabins surrounded by a wooden stockade.

The explorer soon realized that he had chosen a bad location. Fort St. Louis was built on marshland in the heart of Karankawa territory. The Karankawas captured or killed many of the French. The settlement lasted only a few years. In 1687, La Salle was killed when his men staged a mutiny (a revolt against a person in charge). Sometime later, Karankawa warriors overran the fort.

Other Frenchmen continued to settle on the Gulf Coast of Louisiana and Texas. Their colonies thrived until 1763, when France lost most of its American possessions to Great Britain at the end of the French and Indian War (1754–1763). The British claimed almost all French territories east of the Mississippi River, except for New Orleans. Texas remained in Spanish hands.

The Native People

Traditional tribes that lived in Texas included the Alabama, Apache, Atakapan, Bidai, Caddo, Coahuiltecan, Comanche, Choctaw, Coushatta, Hasinai, Jumano, Karankawa, Kickapoo, Kiowa, Tonkawa, and Wichita, though the Comanche were latecomers. They arrived in the area just before the Europeans did. During the early 1800s, however, many more Native Americans moved into Texas, having been pushed out of their traditional lands to the east by American settlement and expansion. These included the Cherokee, Choctaw, Chickasaw, Kickapoo, and Shawnee.

The Native Americans of Texas had been living in the area for more than ten thousand years. Some were hunters and gatherers, nomadic hunters, or farming people by the time Europeans began to arrive in North America. Men's and women's roles varied among these different lifestyles, but women typically harvested *maize* (hard corn), squash, and beans, and also gathered nuts, cactus leaves, and fruit, while men did most of the hunting and fishing along the coast. Children often collected other food, such as berries, nuts, and herbs. In Texas' many areas, Native American groups lived in many different types of houses. Some could be set up quickly and were portable, which made them well suited to a nomadic lifestyle, like the tepee (a conical tent of poles and animal skins). Others were permanent dwellings for farming tribes who couldn't leave their fields or harvests, like the stone and adobe buildings of the pueblos.

Of the many tribes that once existed in Texas, only three remain as relatively intact recognized tribes. The others were exterminated or forced to disband or relocate outside of Texas. Some of these, like the Comanche, fought back against the Europeans, while some disbanded and integrated into Texan society by giving up their tribal ways and affiliations.

There are three federally recognized tribes in Texas. These are the Alabama-Coushatta Tribes of Texas, the Kickapoo Traditional Tribe of Texas (formerly the Texas Band of Traditional Kickapoo), and the Ysleta Del Sur Pueblo of Texas. There are no additional Native American tribes that are recognized by the state in addition to those recognized by the Federal Government.

Spotlight on The Caddo

The name Caddo comes from their own name for themselves, Kadohadacho. The original meaning of that name isn't known for certain. Some Caddo people believe it comes from the native words for "true chiefs."

The Caddo people constructed their homes out of earth and woven grass called thatch.

Distribution: The Caddo are original residents of the southern Plains, particularly Texas, Oklahoma, Arkansas, and Louisiana. Most Caddo people today live in Oklahoma.

Homes: The Caddo in Texas built pole and earthen lodges with roofs of thatched grass. Each Caddo village also included a temple and a sports field. Some villages were surrounded by log walls for protection.

Food: The Caddo were farming people. Caddo women harvested crops of corn, beans, pumpkins, and sunflowers. Caddo men hunted for deer, buffalo, and small game, and went fishing in the rivers. Traditional Caddo foods included cornbread, soups, and stews. The Caddo also removed salt from underground mines to use in their cooking.

Clothing: Caddo Indian men wore breechcloths, sometimes with leather leggings to protect their legs. Caddo women wore wraparound skirts and poncho tops made of woven fiber and deerskin. Both genders wore earrings and moccasins. Caddo men did not usually wear shirts, but in cold weather, both men and women wore buffalo robes.

American Stephen F. Austin asked the Mexican government for permission to found a colony in northeast Texas. Today, Texas's capital, Austin, honors him by bearing his name.

Third Flag: Mexico, 1821–1836

In 1821, Mexico won its independence from Spain. A new flag flew over Texas: the eagle banner of the Mexican nation. The new government was not very interested in Texas. An American named Stephen F. Austin was, however. With the permission of the Mexican government, he started an American colony in northeastern Texas. In return for land, he agreed that the settlers would become citizens of Mexico and obey its laws. Austin himself kept this agreement. He was strict about the type of settlers he would allow in his colony. He wanted to be sure that only the right citizens—those who were serious about creating a successful settlement—moved into the area.

Many settlers were Mexican citizens in name only. They did not understand the culture or the language, and they were not interested in learning. Some settlers from the United States brought slaves to Texas, even though slavery was illegal under Mexican law. It was only a matter of time before conflict between these two very different cultures erupted into a full-scale war.

After the battle of San Jacinto, Mexican general Antonio López de Santa Anna (center in white pants and short blue jacket) was captured by the victorious Texans. General Sam Houston lies injured on the ground in this painting.

Making a Yarn Doll

There was a time when frontier mothers made yarn dolls for their young children, and older kids made them for themselves!

What You Need

Yarn

A piece of sturdy cardboard or a hardcover book to use as a wrapping board (The size of the cardboard/book determines the size of the doll you will make; select a size that is approximately the same size as the finished product you'd like)

Scissors

Choice of decorations (contrasting yarn, ribbon, beads, googly eyes, etc.)

What to Do

- Tape or hold an end of the yarn at the bottom of your wrapping board. Loop the yarn loosely around the wrapping board lengthwise.

- Keep wrapping the yarn around the wrapping board. On the last wrap, end the yarn at the bottom of the wrapping board. The more times you wrap, the thicker the doll will be, and the thickness of the yarn used determines the fullness of the doll. How tall you make your dolls will determine how many times you wrap the body. If you want to make your doll larger or smaller, experiment until you find satisfying proportions. You'll usually need eighty to two hundred wraps.

- Carefully slip a piece of yarn around 10 inches (25.4 cm) long under the yarn at the top of the wrapping board; tie it in a tight knot. Slip the tied yarn off of the wrapping board.

- Tie another piece of string about an inch or more down (depending on length of doll) below the top knot to create a tight, round head.

- Pull out a few loops on each side to be the doll's arms.

- In the middle section of yarn, tie a string tightly where you'd like her/his waist to be.

- Tie the arms at the wrists and trim the looped yarn ends.

- Evenly clip the loops at the bottom of the doll.

- If you want a girl, you now have a skirt. If you want a boy, split the skirt in the center into two parts from the waist down. Tie them off as you did the arms.

- Decorate as desired.

That war began in October 1835, when a group of Texans defeated a Mexican force trying to capture the Texans' cannon at the town of Gonzales, near San Antonio. (Some people liken the Battle of Gonzales to the Battles of Lexington and Concord that started the American Revolution in 1775.) On March 2, 1836, Texas declared independence from Mexico. While Texan leaders met at Washington-on-the-Brazos (the Brazos is a river in Texas), Mexican troops were already besieging the Alamo in San Antonio, which had been captured by Texan forces in December 1835. (The Alamo, originally a mission, had been turned into a fort.) For thirteen days, a force of 190 to 260 Texans held off an army of nearly 2,000 Mexican soldiers. Though all the Texans were killed when Mexican troops launched a full-scale attack on March 6, their heroic stand inspired the Texan forces. "Remember the Alamo!" became a rallying cry for Texas troops.

On April 21, 1836, Sam Houston led an army of Texans against Mexican forces at San Jacinto. Houston knew how to plan a battle. He was able to inspire his soldiers to defeat a much larger force of professional soldiers. The battle lasted only eighteen minutes, and Houston's army won the day. The land they fought on is near what is now the city of Houston. Mexican leader Antonio López de Santa Anna, who was captured after the battle, recognized the independence of Texas, and Sam Houston became a Texas hero.

Fourth Flag: The Republic of Texas, 1836-1845

The now-famous Lone Star banner of Texas became the flag of the new republic. Sam Houston became its first president, and Stephen F. Austin was named its secretary of state.

Texas had no regular army to defend its citizens. Stephen Austin first brought together a group of volunteers, whom he dubbed Rangers, to patrol and protect the area. The Texas Rangers became an officially recognized special police force in 1835. These men were charged with protecting settlers against bandits and Native American raids. Nevertheless, Texas's security remained threatened by Mexico to the south and by Native Americans in the west. To truly gain protection, many Texans believed, Texas would have to become a part of the United States.

In order to become a state, Texas needed to form a stable government. There was another sticking point: slavery was legal in Texas. Some U.S. states that had

Brand New Word

A maverick—a person who does things differently—was defined as such by Samuel A. Maverick, a Texas engineer and rancher in the nineteenth century, because he did not brand his cattle.

The first black people to live in what is now the state of Texas were brought there as slaves. Many stayed in the area even after Emancipation.

abolished slavery did not want to allow Texas to become a state. Nevertheless, in 1845, the U.S. Congress voted to admit Texas to the Union (the United States), and it became the twenty-eighth state.

The Fifth Flag: The United States, 1845–1861 and 1865–Present

When Texas became a state, U.S. president James Polk wanted to secure its southern border at the Rio Grande. Mexico disputed the location of the border. Polk also wanted to bring California and New Mexico, then part of Mexico, into the United States. At the time, "New Mexico" was bigger than the present state with that name. It included the entire American Southwest between Texas and California.

Polk offered to buy Mexican claims in the region, but Mexico refused to sell. It also renounced its recognition of Texas independence. Polk responded by sending American troops to Texas in 1846.

When U.S. troops moved south toward the Rio Grande, into the disputed border territory also claimed by Mexico, Mexican soldiers fired on them. This was, in effect, the first battle of the Mexican-American War, and it was fought on April 25, 1846, on land

In the mid nineteenth century, Texas was a disputed territory, with both the U.S. and Mexican governments claiming authority. The resulting conflict over control is known as the Mexican-American War.

that is now part of Texas. U.S. general Zachary Taylor sent word to President Polk that fighting had begun, and the United States officially declared war on Mexico on May 13. The war ended, with an American victory, almost two years after it began.

The United States and Mexico signed the Treaty of Guadalupe Hidalgo on February 2, 1848. Mexico was forced to give up its claim to Texas and also to give up—or cede—New Mexico and California to the United States in exchange for $15 million.

The end of the war did not stop border fights in the Rio Grande Valley or Native American raids in the west. South and West Texas remained dangerous places for settlers. East Texas, however, was not as violent. It became a vast cotton-growing area, with much of the land owned by white "gentlemen farmers" and worked by black slaves.

The Sixth Flag: The Confederacy, 1861-1865

For the first sixteen years of Texas's statehood, the United States was divided between Southern states

Twister Capitol

Texas gets hit with more than twice as many tornadoes as any other state, mainly in North Texas and the Panhandle. The average number of tornadoes to touch down in Texas each year is 139.

★10★KEY CITIES★ ★ ★

Houston

San Antonio

Austin

1. Houston: population 2,099,451

Houston is the most populous city in Texas with 2,099,451 people, and the fourth most populous city in the United States. It was incorporated as a city in 1837. Houston's **economy** has a broad industrial base in energy, **manufacturing**, aeronautics, and transportation.

2. San Antonio: population 1,327,407

San Antonio, officially the City of San Antonio, was founded as an expansion of a Spanish Mission in 1718. Its economy is focused primarily within military, health care, government civil service, financial services, **oil** and gas, and **tourism** sectors.

3. Dallas: population 1,197,816

Dallas' prominence arose from its historical importance as a center for the oil and cotton industries, and its position along numerous railroad lines. Dallas was founded in 1841 and formally incorporated as a city in February 1856.

4. Austin: population 790,390

Austin is the capital of Texas, was the capital of the independent nation of Texas, and incorporated in 1839. In the late 1800s, Austin is known as the City of the Violet Crown for the wintertime violet glow across the hills just after sunset.

5. Fort Worth: population 741,206

Fort Worth was established in 1849 as an Army outpost on a bluff overlooking the Trinity River. The city is home to Texas Christian University, Texas Wesleyan University, University of North Texas Health Science Center, and Texas A&M University School of Law.

TEXAS ★ ★ ★ ★ ★

Arlington

Corpus Christi

Laredo

6. El Paso: population 649,121

El Paso stands on the Rio Grande, across the border from Juárez, Chihuahua, Mexico, and the two cities form the largest bilingual, binational work force in the Western Hemisphere. El Paso was founded in 1680, and incorporated as a city in 1873.

7. Arlington: population 365,438

Arlington was founded in 1876 along the Texas and Pacific Railway, and was named after General Robert E. Lee's Arlington House in Virginia. Arlington grew as a cotton-ginning and farming center, and incorporated in 1884.

8. Corpus Christi: population 305,215

Corpus Christi is a coastal city in south Texas, and has the nicknames "Texas Riviera" and "Sparkling City by the Sea" because of its location. Today it is the fifth largest U.S. port and deepest inshore port on the Gulf of Mexico.

9. Plano: population 259,841

Plano has been designated the best place to live in the western United States and the eleventh best place to live in the United States by *CNN Money* magazine. It also has been selected as the safest city in America by *Forbes*.

10. Laredo: population 236,091

Founded in 1755, Laredo is the largest inland port on the United States-Mexico border. More than 47 percent of United States trade to Mexico, and more than 36 percent of Mexican trade to the U.S., crosses through Laredo.

that allowed slavery and Northern states where it had been abolished or was never legal. This division was one of the factors that led to the Civil War. In November 1860, Abraham Lincoln was elected president of the United States. Although opposed to slavery, he had said he would not take action as president to end it in the states where it already existed. Still, many people in the South did not want to remain part of the United States. Between December

Native Sons in the White House

Dwight D. Eisenhower became the first person born in Texas to be elected President in 1952. The only other native-born Texan to be elected to our highest office was Lyndon Johnson in 1964. George H. W. Bush was born in Massachusetts, and George W. Bush was born in Connecticut. Both were residents of Texas at the time of their election.

1860 and the spring of 1861, eleven Southern states—including Texas—seceded (withdrew) from the Union and joined together as the Confederate States of America.

From April 1861 to the spring of 1865, Northern troops fought to defeat the Confederacy in order to preserve the Union. Not many battles were fought on Texas soil, but the state contributed sixty thousand soldiers, plus large amounts of ammunition and other supplies to the Confederate army.

The Civil War officially ended in a Union victory when Confederate general Robert E. Lee surrendered to Union general Ulysses S. Grant at Appomattox Court House in Virginia on April 9, 1865. However, the last battle of the war, the Battle of Palmito Ranch, was fought in the Lone Star State near Brownsville more than a month later, on May 13, by troops that had not gotten the news of Lee's surrender. A "state of peace" was declared between the Union and most Southern states on April 2, 1866. A similar proclamation between the United States and Texas was not issued until August 20, 1866.

For the second half of the 1860s, Texas was under the control of a U.S. military government. To be readmitted to the Union as states, the states of the former Confederacy had to meet several requirements. Each state had to construct a new state constitution and ratify the Thirteenth, Fourteenth, and Fifteenth amendments to the U.S. Constitution, all of which had been added after the Civil War. (The Thirteenth Amendment abolished slavery; the Fourteenth guaranteed all people equal protection under the law; and the Fifteenth gave black men the right to vote.) After meeting the necessary requirements, Texas was readmitted to the Union in 1870.

Before railroads reached across the expanse of Texas, it was cowboys who were expected to lead herds of tens of thousands of cattle from Texas ranches to Kansas or Missouri railroad lines. Cowboys were so important that they remain an important symbol of the state.

Cowboys and Cattle Drives

In the second half of the nineteenth century, cattle raising became increasingly important in the wide open spaces of West Texas, where there was enough grazing land to support large herds. Before railroads reached many parts of Texas in the 1880s, in order to get their cattle to market, ranchers and the cowboys who worked for them organized huge annual cattle drives. The men would spend days branding their cattle and rounding them up for the long walk to the nearest railroad station. They often covered distances of up to one thousand miles to reach railroad lines in Kansas or Missouri.

A Friendly State

Texas is called the Lone Star State because of the design of its flag, which prominently features one white star. The name Texas (or Tejas) comes from a Caddo Indian word that means "friends" or "allies." Perhaps that explains the state's motto: friendship.

Hundreds of thousands of animals were moved to market each year in these cattle drives.

The age of the cattle drives to northern and western markets lasted only about twenty years. They were made unnecessary when railroads and refrigeration reached the region in the 1880s. The first big year for the drives was 1866, when an estimated 260,000 head of cattle were taken across the Red River.

The drives normally started in the spring after the cattle roundup. Grass was still available on the route at that time to feed the herd, allowing them to be delivered before cold weather set in. A crew of twelve men could drive a herd of two thousand to three thousand cattle. While herds were made up of livestock from several owners, all of the animals were branded with the same road brand. The drive could cover 10 to 15 miles (16 to 24 km) per day, so a drive to Kansas could take one hundred days.

The second most important man on a cattle drive, after the trail boss, was the cook. The legendary Charles Goodnight invented the chuck wagon in 1866 for the cook to use to feed his crews. Goodnight also developed a wagon for transporting calves, which were too small to keep up with the others on the drive.

West Texas was a somewhat lawless area at this time. The slow-moving herds were often easy prey for outlaws, such as cattle rustlers (thieves). These outlaws were usually cowboys who knew how to ride horses and rope cattle, and were familiar with the countryside. The Texas Rangers, legendary for their horsemanship and their marksmanship, were the main defenders of law and order in many areas. In Texas at this time, if a person was caught rustling cattle, he might be hanged.

The Twentieth Century and Beyond

Texas began the twentieth century with a major discovery. In 1901, mining engineer A. F. Lucas struck oil at Spindletop. When the "gusher" shot into the air, it changed American industry. According to geologist Michael T. Halbouty, Spindletop "started the liquid fuel age, which brought forth the automobile, the airplane, the network of highways…[and] untold comforts and conveniences."

When the United States entered World War I in 1917, the army found that the wide open spaces of Texas were ideal locations for training bases. Soldiers from all over the country went to Texas. Men also went to Kelly Field in San Antonio to learn how to fly. It was the first base for training pilots to fly the new airplanes that would be dogfighting in the skies of Europe. (A dogfight is an air battle between planes.) The base was expanded during World War II (in which the United States fought from 1941 to 1945). It was used to train a new generation of pilots for a new generation of military planes. (Until Kelly Air

The NASA space center in Houston, Texas, helped guide Apollo 11 astronauts Neil Armstrong, Michael Collins, and Buzz Aldrin. The mission was a great success, making America the first country to land humans on the Moon.

Force Base closed on July 13, 2001, it was the U.S. military's oldest continuously operating air base.)

By 1961, people were ready to fly even farther. The National Aeronautics and Space Administration (NASA) opened a space center in Houston. There, NASA scientists and engineers designed and developed the spacecraft and managed the missions that took American astronauts into space. In 1969, ground controllers in Houston worked with astronauts aboard the Apollo 11 spacecraft—men who became the first humans to land and walk on the Moon.

Texas became a national presence in politics by sending three Texans to the White House in the second half of the twentieth and

Taylor's Like Ike

U.S. general Zachary Taylor, who became a military hero during the Mexican-American War, would become the twelfth president of the United States in 1849. General Dwight David Eisenhower of Texas was also a war hero before being elected president: he was the supreme commander of Allied forces for Western Europe during World War II.

Districts across Texas sought to integrate their schools during the 1955–1956 school year.

early twenty-first centuries. Lyndon B. Johnson served as president from 1963 to 1969. George H. W. Bush served from 1989 to 1993. His son, George W. Bush, served from 2001 to 2009. A fourth president, Dwight D. Eisenhower, who served from 1953 to 1961, was born in Texas, though he grew up in Kansas.

In Texas, as in other states, racial segregation divided people. In the later part of the nineteenth century and continuing through much of the twentieth, laws and regulations prohibited African Americans from attending the same schools and using the same public facilities as whites. Ethel Minor of the National Association for the Advancement of Colored People (NAACP) recalled, "'Colored only' signs were everywhere. There were a lot of places where we weren't allowed to try on clothes."

The civil rights movement was a nationwide social action campaign begun in the 1950s to gain equal rights for African Americans. It included marches and demonstrations, acts of public protest, and court cases brought to overturn segregation laws and practices. One landmark Texas case in 1950 opened the doors of the University of Texas law school to an African American student for the first time. This happened four years before the historic U.S. Supreme Court decision that outlawed racial segregation in schools all over the country.

The struggle for equal rights continued through the twentieth century and came to include Mexican Americans and other groups besides African Americans. Activist Thomas C. Rockeymoore of the Texas NAACP spoke of the importance of ending inequality when he said, "Discrimination affects all of us, no matter what race you happen to be."

In Their Own Words

"[N]o frontiersman who has no other occupation than that of hunter will be received—no drunkard, no gambler, no profane swearer, no idler."

—Stephen F. Austin on the type of settlers he wanted for Texas

Texas played a large role in the passing of the Civil Rights Act in 1964. However, its part came about because of one of the saddest incidents in the history of the state and of the nation.

Lyndon Baines Johnson was born in Stonewall, Texas, in 1908 and was elected to the United States Senate in 1848. In 1953, he became the youngest minority leader (the head of the party with fewer senators) in U.S. Senate history. When the Democrats gained control of the Senate in 1954, he became the majority leader.

Johnson ran for president in 1960 but lost the Democratic nomination to John F. Kennedy, a war hero from Massachusetts. Johnson had strong support in the South, so Kennedy selected him as his vice presidential running mate. Together, they won the election.

On November 22, 1963, President Kennedy was riding in a motorcade through Dallas when he was killed by a sniper's bullet. Texas governor John Connally was also wounded in the car, but he recovered completely from his wounds. Vice President Johnson, who had been riding in a vehicle two cars behind Kennedy and was completely unhurt in the incident, was sworn in as the thirty-sixth president of the United States aboard Air Force One, the president's airplane, as it flew back to Washington, DC.

As vice president, Johnson had worked closely with President Kennedy on equal rights for minorities. Continuing this important goal, President Johnson pushed a landmark civil rights bill proposed by Kennedy through Congress before the next election. Several key points in this bill included:

- The outlawing of discrimination in theaters, motels, restaurants, and other public accommodations

- The outlawing of different voting rules for people of different races and economic status

- The authorization of the withdrawal of federal funds from programs that practiced discrimination

- The encouragement of the desegregation of public schools and giving the U. S. Attorney General the authorization to file lawsuits to force desegregation

- The outlawing of discrimination in employment in any business with more than twenty-five workers and establishment of the Equal Employment Opportunity Commission

Before he signed the bill on July 2, 1964, Johnson said: "We believe that all men are created equal—yet many are denied equal treatment. We believe that all men have certain inalienable rights. We believe that all men are entitled to the blessings of liberty—yet millions are being deprived of those blessings, not because of their own failures, but because of the color of their skins.

Home of the Dome

Houston was the site of the first domed stadium, the Astrodome, which was called "the eighth wonder of the world" when it opened in 1965. The grass inside died, however, forcing the Colt 45s to play the last two weeks of baseball season on painted dirt. Artificial grass, or AstroTurf, was developed and installed for the 1966 season.

"The reasons are deeply embedded in history and tradition and the nature of man. We can understand without rancor or hatred how all this happens. But it cannot continue. Our Constitution, the foundation of our Republic, forbids it. The principles of our freedom forbid it. Morality forbids it. And the law I sign tonight forbids it..."

Johnson won reelection in 1964, but was faced with many problems to address in addition to racial discrimination. The biggest of these was the Vietnam War, which escalated during his administration. However, he was able to establish two federal programs that continue to help a lot of people: Medicare and Medicaid.

10 KEY DATES IN STATE HISTORY

1. April 30, 1598

Juan de Oñate plants the Spanish flag on Texas soil.

2. August 24, 1821

Mexico gains independence from Spain after a ten-year war, ending three hundred years of Spanish rule in Mexico. Texas becomes part of Mexico.

3. March 2, 1836

Texas declares its independence from Mexico and becomes a republic. Independence is secured on April 21 when Texas troops rout a larger force of Mexican troops to win the battle of San Jacinto.

4. December 29, 1845

Texas joins the United States as the twenty-eighth state, one year after the U.S. Congress agrees to annex the territory of Texas.

5. February 15, 1876

The present state constitution is adopted, nearly six years after Texas was readmitted to the Union on March 30, 1870.

6. September 8, 1900

A hurricane and storm surge destroy 3,600 homes and kill up to 8,000 people in Galveston, one of the worst natural disasters in U.S. history.

7. January 10, 1901

An oil discovery at Spindletop, near Beaumont, thrusts Texas into the petroleum age.

8. September 19, 1961

NASA announces plans for the Manned Spacecraft Center in Houston, which opened in 1963 and was later called the Johnson Space Center.

9. November 22, 1963

President John F. Kennedy is assassinated in Dallas, and Texas governor John Connolly was wounded. Vice President Lyndon Johnson of Texas is sworn in as president.

10. November 7, 2000

George W. Bush is elected the forty-third U.S. president. He serves two terms.

"Big Tex," a 55-foot- (16 m) tall statue of a cowboy, has greeted visitors to the State Fair of Texas in Dallas since 1952.

The People

There is an old saying that Texas is not just a state of the Union; it is a state of mind. In other words, being from Texas is somehow special. Texans come from many different backgrounds. People of Native American, Mexican, and African American descent have helped to shape the state. Other cultures have also added to the mix, including people of German, Czech, Irish, Italian, and Vietnamese heritage. Some people outside Texas are unaware of this cultural variety. To them, Texas means one thing: cowboys.

Cowboy Ways

From the Dallas Cowboys of the National Football League to the 55-foot- (16 m) tall "Big Tex" statue at the state fairground, Texans love cowboys. The modern cowboy no longer has gunfights in the middle of a dusty Texas street or rides along the Chisholm Trail—a cattle trail that led from Texas to Kansas—with a herd of longhorn cattle. He might be a cattle rancher with a college degree in livestock management. He might be a professional rodeo performer or an accountant or a computer programmer who likes to wear western boots and ten-gallon hats. The legend of the tough-as-nails wrangler who lived by the code of the West is part of Texan's heritage. Keeping it alive is a way of honoring the past.

Mexican Americans

According to U.S. Census Bureau estimates, in 2012 more than one-third of Texans (38 percent) were of **Hispanic** origin. People of Mexican descent make up the largest Hispanic group in the state. They are concentrated in the south, near the Mexican border. Many of these people live in poor neighborhoods called *barrios* or *colonias*.

Good jobs are not easy to find in the barrio. Sooner or later, many people who live there end up working in the fields. Each year, migrant farm workers go from farm to farm, following the harvest northward as far as Minnesota. The work is hard, and the wages are low.

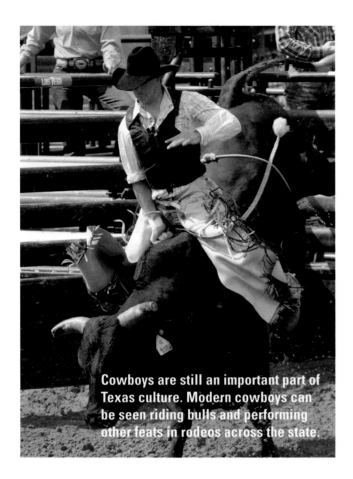

Cowboys are still an important part of Texas culture. Modern cowboys can be seen riding bulls and performing other feats in rodeos across the state.

Mexican Americans in Texas have created their own subculture. It is a blend of Mexico and Texas, known as *Tejano* (Tay-HAN-oh). The word, like the people it describes, is a blend of "Texan" and "Méxicano." Outside the Mexican American community, Tejano culture is best known for its music.

Singer Selena Quintanilla-Pérez won Female Vocalist of the Year at the Tejano Music Awards in 1986 when she was only sixteen. Selena's popularity as a Tejano singer led to recognition in other areas of the music world. Her popularity was on the rise across America when Selena was murdered in 1995. She is a member of the South Texas Music Walk of Fame and in 2001 was inducted into the Tejano R.O.O.T.S. Hall of Fame.

African Americans

The first African Americans in Texas were brought in as slaves. After the Civil War, they struggled to make a place for themselves as free people in a free society. Some moved west and found work as cowboys. Others became sharecroppers where a person farmed a parcel of land and was paid with a portion, or share, of the crop. Most landlords took advantage of black workers and created a system that kept the sharecroppers in poverty.

Black people who tried to find employment in other areas were paid less than whites that held the same jobs.

This system of inequality spilled over into every area of life. Segregation, and what was known as the black codes, kept black people separated from white society. Black people were required to go to separate schools from whites and to use separate facilities, such as restrooms, water fountains, waiting rooms, and the like. In all

Late Arriving News

Although the Emancipation Proclamation was issued in 1863, the news didn't reach Texas until Union troops arrived in Galveston on June 19, 1865. When they learned of their freedom, African Americans reacted with joy, and the occasion is now remembered as Juneteenth. It is the oldest nationally celebrated commemoration of the ending of African-American slavery.

cases, facilities used by blacks were inferior to those used by whites. In the schools for African American children, for example, students were taught with outdated textbooks and had to make due with old, often broken, lab and playground equipment. Tejanos faced similar discrimination. It was not until the civil rights movement of the 1950s and 1960s that African Americans began to see significant improvements in their lives.

This mural in San Antonio's historic Market Square celebrates Mexican culture, which has been an important part of Texas's history for centuries.

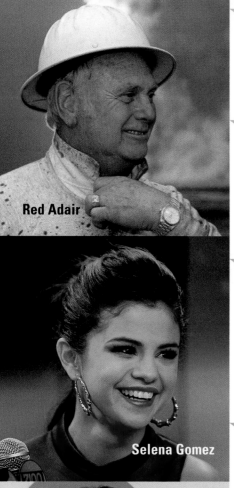

Red Adair

Selena Gomez

Beyoncé

1. Red Adair

Paul "Red" Adair, who was born in Houston in 1915, specialized in putting out oil well fires, which start deep in the earth, fueled by huge supplies of oil or natural gas.

2. Elizabeth Coleman

Elizabeth "Bessie" Coleman was born in 1892 and was the first female pilot of African American descent and the first person of African American descent to hold an international pilot license

3. Selena Gomez

This singer and actress from Grand Prairie started her entertainment career when she joined *Barney & Friends* at age twelve. She has since appeared in several television series for the Disney Channel, including the *Wizards of Waverly Place*, and has starred in several movies.

4. Buddy Holly

Buddy Holly was born in Lubbock in 1936. He and his bandmates in the Crickets were among the first rock musicians to write their own songs. Thanks to hits such as "That'll Be the Day" and "Peggy Sue," Holly was an incredibly popular and influential musician.

5. Beyoncé Giselle Knowles-Carter

Beyoncé is a singer and actress who was born in 1981 and raised in Houston, Texas. She rose to fame in the late 1990s as lead singer of R&B girl-group Destiny's Child, and has moved on to a successful solo career.

6. Chester Nimitz

This war hero from Fredericksburg was appointed Commander in Chief, Pacific Fleet and Pacific Ocean Areas. He led the fleet to crucial victories during World War II, and was promoted to fleet admiral, the highest grade in the navy.

7. Sandra Day O'Connor

The first female Supreme Court Justice was born in El Paso in 1930. O'Connor was elected twice to the Arizona state senate. She was appointed to the Supreme Court by President Ronald Reagan in 1981, and retired in 2006.

8. Robert Rodriguez

Robert Rodriguez is best known for his *Spy Kids* movie trilogy. The filmmaker, who was born in 1968 in San Antonio, shoots and produces many films in Texas and Mexico. Rodriguez is also a writer, cinematographer, and composer.

9. Richard Smalley

Richard Smalley is considered the father of nanotechnology (molecular level robots and machinery). He won the Nobel Prize in Chemistry in 1996 for his discovery of fullerenes, which are any molecule composed entirely of carbon, in the form of a hollow sphere, ellipsoid, tube, and many other shapes.

10. Chesley Burnett Sullenberger, III

"Sully" Sullenberger, who was born in Denison, is a retired airline captain. He successfully executed an emergency water landing of US Airways Flight 1549, after the aircraft was disabled by striking a flock of geese during its initial climb out of LaGuardia Airport in 2009.

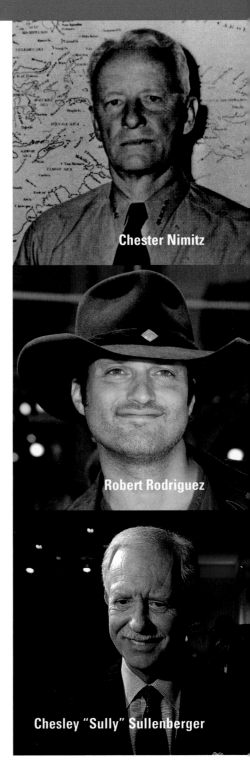

Chester Nimitz

Robert Rodriguez

Chesley "Sully" Sullenberger

Who Texans Are

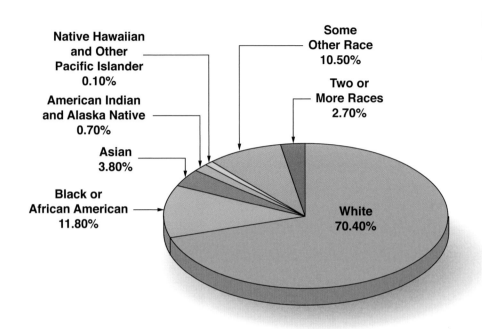

Native Hawaiian and Other Pacific Islander
0.10%

American Indian and Alaska Native
0.70%

Asian
3.80%

Black or African American
11.80%

Some Other Race
10.50%

Two or More Races
2.70%

White
70.40%

Total Population
25,145,561

Hispanic or Latino (of any race):

• 9,460,921 people (37.60%)

Note: The pie chart shows the racial breakdown of the state's population based on the categories used by the U.S. Bureau of the Census. The Census Bureau reports information for Hispanics or Latinos separately, since they may be of any race. Percentages in the pie chart may not add to 100 because of rounding.

Source: U.S. Bureau of the Census, 2010 Census

In the mid-twentieth century, Texas had a population shift. People began leaving farms and rural towns for cities. Large numbers of African Americans joined in this move. Today, more than 40 percent of black Texans live in the urban areas of Dallas and Houston.

Native Americans

Dozens of Native American tribes once made Texas their home. Today, there are only three federally recognized tribes in the state: the Texas Band Kickapoo, the Alabama-Coushatta, and the Ysleta del Sur Pueblo.

The Alabamas and Coushattas are both members of the Upper Creek Confederacy of Indians and are of the Muskogean Nation. They share a **reservation** in the Big Thicket region in southeast Texas. Sam Houston originally gave the land to these tribes as thanks for their generosity in caring for settlers who passed through their villages.

The Tigua of Ysleta del Sur Pueblo in El Paso County are the last Pueblo people in Texas. Pueblo is the Spanish word for "town." The Texas Tiguas originally came from a pueblo in New Mexico, which was already well established when the Spanish first visited it in 1539. Although the Tiguas have lived in West Texas since the 1670s, they were not officially called a Native American tribe until 1968. Ysleta del Sur Pueblo is the oldest community in the state of Texas, and the Tigua Tribal Council is the oldest government in the state.

Native Americans keep their traditions alive by participating in powwows, such as this one in Fredericksburg.

The Kickapoos once lived in the central Great Lakes region. As a result of conflicts with European settlers, they migrated to Kansas, Oklahoma, and Texas. Although the Kickapoos have a reservation in southeast Texas, they enjoy a sort of dual citizenship with Mexico. They are free to move back and forth across the border to live or work.

Many Native Americans are no longer able to live their people's traditional way of life. Still, many of these groups have found ways to keep their culture alive through museums, education programs, and powwows. At a powwow, native peoples gather to share traditional foods and crafts, and to take part in ceremonies that have been passed down from generation to generation.

Other Texans

In the nineteenth century, many European **immigrants** settled in Texas. Today, some of their descendants enjoy keeping old-country traditions alive. For example, there is the German singing society in San Antonio and the Italian-American cultural society in El Paso. Every year, the Irish music festival draws big crowds to the state fairground in Dallas.

People of Vietnamese descent are among the newest Texans. After the Vietnam War ended in 1975, many Vietnamese refugees came to the United States. More than 52,000 immigrants from Vietnam chose to settle in Texas. They set up communities in cities such as Dallas, Houston, and Austin, and along the Gulf Coast.

Traditional Irish step dancers perform at the annual Irish music festival in Dallas.

Undocumented Immigration: A Texas Issue

Each year, thousands of undocumented immigrants come to Texas and other southwestern states. These are people who do not have the required documents issued by the U.S. government allowing them to live permanently in the United States. They come mostly from Mexico, though many travel through Mexico from Central and South America. Most are desperately poor people who come seeking work.

Trying to enter the United States without a passport or other legal papers is dangerous. Some people try to walk across the border in remote desert areas to avoid being caught by U.S. Border Patrol agents. There is a great deal of controversy about these people. Some are outraged at the use of schools and other government services by people who are not legal residents of the United States. They also feel that undocumented immigrants take jobs from legal residents. Others argue that their labor contributes to the U.S. economy.

Many immigrants pay smugglers to help them cross the border. Some of these smugglers simply steal the money without taking anyone over the border. Others may transport people in unsafe, cruel conditions. In one case, Border Patrol officers heard pounding from inside a truck and found 113 people crammed together inside. In other cases, people have died from the heat and shortage of air inside the trucks sneaking them over the border.

The United States government is working to encourage people who want to move to the United States to go through the legal process for entering the country. The U.S. Department of Homeland Security has increased patrols and built hundreds of miles of new fencing along the border to prevent people from simply walking in.

Thousands of undocumented immigrants from Central and South America make a dangerous journey to the United States in search better lives across the border every year. Many are caught at the Texas border by U.S. Border Patrol agents.

Law enforcement officials are cracking down on smugglers and on people who knowingly hire undocumented workers, which is against federal law. State and local governments are trying to deal with the money issues, while social welfare agencies deal with the human ones, such as poverty and abuse.

An influx of migrant children created a crisis in the summer of 2014; fifty thousand unaccompanied youths had crossed illegally into the United States in the previous eight months, double the amount from the previous year. Many came from Central America. This overwhelmed border agents and strained the budgets of groups that provide food and housing.

Undocumented immigration is just one of the controversial social issues that Texans will have to handle in the twenty-first century.

In Their Own Words

"My little sister always gets scared when we see immigration [officials are] out in Beaumont cause she knows what will happen if they catch us. I would really like to go to college here and get a good education. . . . I cry my eyes out some days 'cause my dad wants a good job. There was one month where we didn't eat anything but noodles cause he hadn't worked for a month."

—Jonathan, an undocumented immigrant from Mexico

Dickens on the Strand

Houston Livestock Show and Rodeo

1. Cinco de Mayo

On May 5, 1862, five thousand Mexican troops defeated a French army of eight thousand. Today, Cinco de Mayo (Spanish for "fifth of May") fiestas celebrate that victory. The largest festival in Austin lasts four days, with music, pageants, and carnival rides.

2. Dickens on the Strand

On the first weekend in December, the Strand National Historic Landmark District in Galveston transforms itself into the Victorian London of author Charles Dickens. People dressed in costumes of the late 1800s gather to watch jugglers, magicians, acrobats, and dancers.

3. Fiesta San Antonio

Every April, this eleven-day fiesta celebrates the battles of the Alamo and San Jacinto, which won independence for Texas in 1836. Events include parades, concerts, and art exhibits.

4. Houston Livestock Show and Rodeo

Every February and March, organizations such as the Future Farmers of America (FFA) come to show animals they have raised and compete for prizes. The second-largest rodeo in the country, it features bronco and bull riding, calf roping, steer wrestling, and barrel racing.

5. Katy Jazz Festival

Held at Katy High School, the festival features an incredible array of jazz performances, master classes, and ARTkaty (a visual arts exhibit and sales). The event is designed to benefit participating students and educators.

TEXAS ★ ★ ★ ★ ★ ★

6. Kolache Festival

This annual festival in Caldwell has been held for almost thirty years. Buleson County was basically a Czech settlement whose people realized their identity was slipping away. Kolache, a Czech wedding pastry, is a favorite national dessert throughout the Czech Republic.

7. Pasadena Strawberry Festival

The Pasadena Strawberry Festival celebrates the first big business in the city. The region's strawberries are famous for their size and sweetness. These strawberries earned Pasadena the title "Strawberry Capital of the South."

8. San Angelo's Children's Fair

At the San Angelo's Children's Fair in April, more than 120 food, game, and activity booths are set up at the park for families to enjoy. All booths are run by non-profit groups and agencies benefiting children's programs.

9. South by Southwest

This annual Austin event is really three festivals: one for film, one for music, and another for interactive technology. They run consecutively over two weeks in March. Attendance has grown from seven hundred in 1987 to more than seventy thousand in 2013.

10. State Fair of Texas

The Texas state fair is the largest in the nation, with more than three million people attending every year. The event is held on a 277-acre (112-hectare) fairground outside Dallas, and includes livestock exhibitions, rides, concerts, fireworks, and a parade.

Kolache Festival

State Fair of Texas

The Texas Capitol in Austin is the largest capitol building in the United States. It is taller than even the U.S. Capitol in Washington, D.C.

How the Government Works

The current Texas constitution was adopted February 15, 1876. Although it has been amended, or changed, hundreds of times, the constitution remains the basic law of the state and sets out the framework for state and local government.

The state government deals with broad issues that affect all of Texas. It makes laws that everyone in the state must obey, and establishes policies in areas such as education, health care, and social welfare.

The Texas state government has three branches: executive, legislative, and judicial. The governor is the chief executive of the state. The legislature makes its laws, and the courts settle legal disputes and try criminals.

Many policies and programs are established at the state level and carried out by counties and cities. Texas has 254 counties, each governed by a commissioners' court. Counties provide services ranging from schools and public hospitals to libraries, jails, and parks. A county sheriff is responsible for law enforcement.

Both the American flag and the Texas state flag fly atop the Capitol in Austin.

Branches of Government

EXECUTIVE

The governor, the head of the executive branch, is elected for a four-year term. He or she can call special sessions of the legislature, appoint members of boards and commissions, and veto (reject) or approve bills passed by the legislature.

LEGISLATIVE

Like the U.S. Congress, the Texas legislature is divided into two houses—a senate and a house of representatives. The senate has thirty-one members, elected for four-year terms. The house has 150 members, who serve two-year terms. Both houses must approve a bill before it goes to the governor for final action.

JUDICIAL

The judicial branch includes different levels of courts, which deal with two kinds of cases: criminal and civil. In a criminal case, someone is accused of a crime and may be sent to prison if convicted. Civil cases involve lawsuits in which one party seeks money from another. Most cases are first heard in a district court. District court decisions can be challenged in a court of appeals. Court of appeals decisions can be appealed to the Texas supreme court (civil cases) or to the court of criminal appeals. Each of these highest courts in the state has nine judges, elected to six-year terms.

There are more than one thousand city, town, and village governments in Texas. These governments usually have an elected council. In some cities, an elected mayor is the head of the local government. In others, a professional city manager is hired to do this work.

At the national level, as in every state, Texas has two senators in the U.S. Congress in Washington, D.C. As of 2014, the Lone Star State had thirty-six members in the U.S. House of Representatives.

Bilingual Education: A Texas Issue

Texas lawmakers have struggled with the issue of bilingual education for years. In a state that has such a large Spanish-speaking population, it is an important issue.

At one time, Texas schools banned students from speaking Spanish while on school grounds. In some schools, students they had to pay a small fine each time they broke the "no Spanish" rule. In others, they were smacked on the hand with a ruler, pinched, pulled by the ear, or had their mouths washed out with soap.

In 1998, state senator Carlos Truan could still remember a time in the 1940s when he was spanked for speaking Spanish on the playground. A Mexican-American student named Edgar said in the 1960s, "A teacher comes up to you and tells you, 'No, no. You know that is a filthy language, nothing but bad words and bad thoughts in that language.' I mean, they are telling you that your language is bad. . . Your mother and father speak a bad language, you speak a bad language. . . That really stuck in my mind."

In 1973, the Bilingual Education and Training Act ended these policies. It required bilingual education in schools where twenty or more students in any one grade spoke

Texas boasts the highest number of bilingual schools in the nation.

limited English. School districts rushed to develop programs. They had to find teachers who could teach mathematics, social studies, and science in Spanish. In 2012, Texas led the nation in number of schools—about 700—using dual-language programs in the elementary grades.

How a Bill Becomes a Law

Citizens in Texas can play a key part in this decision-making. If a citizen has an idea for a law, he or she can suggest it to representatives in the general assembly. Sometimes voters will collect many signatures from other voters who share their opinions on an idea. Then they present this petition about a proposed law to legislators. Members of the general assembly also come up with ideas for new laws.

A proposed law is called a bill. Wherever the idea originates, a representative or person on the representative's staff takes the idea and writes a bill. A bill can be introduced in the house of representatives or in the senate. If the bill starts in the house of representatives, the president of the house of representatives assigns a committee to review the bill. The members of the committee hold hearings and discuss the bill. They may make many revisions. If they agree that the bill should be a law, they present it to the house of representatives. The entire house then votes on the bill. If it is approved by a majority vote, it is sent to the state senate. The senate follows a procedure similar to the one in the house of representatives. A committee considers the bill, and if it is approved by the committee, then the entire senate votes on it.

When both parts of the legislature have approved a bill, it is sent to the governor. If the governor approves, the bill becomes a law. However, if the governor rejects, or

Citizens sit in the gallery while the Texas House of Representatives holds session.

vetoes, the bill, the house and senate still have a chance to pass it. If the house and senate both vote in favor of the bill again, this time by a two-thirds majority, the governor's veto can be overturned, and the bill becomes a law.

In 1997, another important education law was passed. It was intended to adapt achievement tests for disabled students. Its progress through the legislature is an example of the law-making process in Texas.

Two Governors in One

Miriam "Ma" Ferguson became the first female governor of Texas in 1924, running after her husband, Jim Ferguson, was impeached, or thrown out of office, for misapplication of public funds. Miriam won another term in 1932 and served until 1935. Fifty-five years later, Texas elected its second female governor, Ann Richards.

HB ("House Bill") 1800, as it was first called, came before the house of representatives on February 27, 1997. It was meant to give students in special-education classes a fair chance to show their skills. Most of the testing changes are a matter of common sense. For example, a blind student cannot be expected to do well on tests that use visual directions and a hearing-impaired student cannot be expected to do well on tests that involve listening.

On March 3, a summary of HB 1800 was read before the full house. It was then sent to the House Committee on Public Education for study. The committee went over it point by point, suggesting changes and asking questions. It held public hearings, which any interested citizen could attend.

When the study was completed, the committee sent the bill back to the full house. After more public readings and debate, the house passed HB 1800 and sent it to the senate. There it went through the same process of readings, reports, and debates. On May 21, the senate passed the bill. On June 17, 1997, the governor signed HB 1800 into law.

By that time, this fairly simple bill had gone through forty-five different actions. If it had been more complicated or more controversial, the process most likely would have taken longer and included more actions. There is a good reason for all this complexity. In Texas, as in other states, the procedure for passing a law includes a number of safeguards. They help to ensure the full and free debate that is the basis of the democratic process.

In the lengthy process of lawmaking, citizen participation helps ensure that Texas government pays attention to the needs of the people. In any democracy that is the greatest goal of the political process.

★ Lyndon B. Johnson: President of the United States, 1963-1969

Born near Stonewall in 1908, Johnson became president of the United States under terrible circumstances. He took the oath of office just hours after President John F. Kennedy was assassinated on November 22, 1963.

★ Barbara Jordan: United States Representative, 1972-1979

This Houston native became the first African American woman to be elected to the Texas state senate in 1966. As a member of the U.S. House Judiciary Committee, she called for the impeachment of President Richard Nixon. Jordan received the Presidential Medal of Freedom from President Bill Clinton in 1994.

★ Sam Rayburn: United States Representative, 1912-1961

Sam Rayburn worked as a teacher and a lawyer before serving six years in the Texas House of Representatives. He was elected to Congress in 1912 and served for forty-eight years and eight months. He was also Speaker of the House for a record seventeen years.

TEXAS
YOU CAN MAKE A DIFFERENCE

Contacting Lawmakers

The contact information for Texas' governor, members of the general assembly, and representatives in the U.S. Congress is available online. Many legislators have individual websites or Facebook pages so that they can keep in touch with their constituents.

For information about the governor and how to contact the governor, visit:

governor.state.tx.us

For names, phone numbers and email addresses for local Texas legislators (in the State House and Senate), visit:

House: www.house.state.tx.us/members/find-your-representative

Senate: www.senate.state.tx.us/75r/Senate/Members.htm#FYI

To find out who represents an area in the Federal government in Washington D.C. as a congressman or senator, visit:

www.govtrack.us/congress/members/TX

Taking on Tests

Many laws are brought about by regular people (including kids) who see a community problem that could be fixed with a new law. By bringing concerns and ideas to the attention of a representative, new laws can be crafted or old laws amended to take care of the problem.

In 2013, a new law, HB5, was passed in the Texas Legislature. This new law aims to save Texas millions of dollars by limiting state-mandated standardized tests. HB5 limits state-mandated tests to English I, English II, algebra I, biology, and U.S. history, and two optional tests (Algebra II and English III) can be administered at the school districts' option.

The idea was introduced to lawmakers by regular Texans, and aided by Texans Advocating for Meaningful Student Assessment (TAMSA), which put pressure on lawmakers by educating people and getting them to write, call, and email their representatives.

Texas leads the United States in oil production. Texas refineries including this one in Galveston Bay can produce up to 4.8 million barrels of oil per day.

Making a Living

For many years, the Texas economy could be described in three words: cows, cotton, and crude (oil). From the vast cattle ranches of the west to the oil fields, farmland, and forests of the east, Texans made a living from the state's abundant natural resources.

Today, the economy is more varied. Texas factories produce everything from children's clothes to vacuum cleaners and clock radios. Technology firms have turned Central Texas into a high-tech center some call the "Silicon Valley of the South." (Silicon Valley is an area near San Francisco, California, known for its concentration of computer and technology firms.) Even so, Texas still ranks top among the states in many of its most traditional industries, including ranching and oil production.

Agriculture

Texas produces a wealth of agricultural products. In 2012, income from these products was about $20 billion. Half of this comes from beef, as the state routinely leads the nation in raising cattle. Cotton is the number-one field crop, followed by hay, corn, wheat, and sorghum grain. Many of the top crops are grown as feed for the cattle industry.

Other agricultural products include milk, chickens, eggs, potatoes, rice, and watermelons. Texas ranks among the five states that grow the most tree crops, such as grapefruits, oranges, and pecans.

Cotton was first grown in Texas by Spanish missionaries. Today, cotton remains a major export, with Texas producing 4.5 million bales per year—the most of any state.

Mining and Mineral Extraction

On January 10, 1901, a domed hill in southeastern Texas made history. Oil drillers had been working at Spindletop for weeks, with no results. That January morning did not begin well. Mud oozed up from the ground, filling the hole and getting in the way of the drill pipe.

Geologist Pete Nester explained what happened next: "After a short time, the…workers set about to clean up the mess… All of a sudden, a noise like a cannon shot came from the hole, and mud came shooting out of the ground like a rocket. Within a few seconds, natural gas, then oil followed…rising to a height of more than 150 feet (46 m). This was more oil than had ever been seen anywhere in the entire world."

That day marked the beginning of another Texas industry.

Role Model

Texas has been a role model for other states in how to attract business. According to one business magazine, Florida's governor said he copied methods used in Texas to attract business. This worked so well that the Sunshine State has moved up to second in one ranking of the best states to do business.

Geologist Pete Nester uncovered a rich oil deposit at Spindletop Hill in Beaumont, Texas. The discovery would change Texas—and the United States—forever.

Hundreds of wells were drilled in the Spindletop area, and in 1902, 17.5 million barrels of oil were pumped out of the ground. The oil fields at Spindletop helped make the United States, for many years, the world's largest producer of oil. More than a century after the Spindletop discovery, the United States was still the world's third-largest oil producer. In 2013, Texas accounted for more than a third of all oil produced in the U.S., more than any other state. If Texas were a country, it would be the world's fourteenth largest oil producer.

Manufacturing

Texas manufacturing began with industries related to natural products: food-processing plants, textile (cloth) mills, and oil refineries. It expanded to include a wide variety of manufactured products, such as shoes, cars, and electronics.

In the 1990s, factory production decreased in industrial states such as Ohio, Pennsylvania, and New York. In Texas, it grew. By 2012, Texas ranked second only to California in the size of its manufacturing workforce.

High-Tech Texas

"High-tech" has come to stand for modern information and communication technologies. In a sense, the entire industry was born in Texas on September 12, 1958. On that day, electrical engineer Jack Kilby demonstrated his new invention: the microchip, or

Aerospace and Aviation

Agriculture

Computers and Communications

1. Aerospace and Aviation

The National Aeronautics and Space Administration's Johnson Space Center is located in Houston. Big companies such as Lockheed Martin, Bell Aerospace, Raytheon, Boeing, and Gulfstream Aerospace employ many of the 200,000 Texans working in this industry.

2. Agriculture

Nearly one in seven jobs in Texas is in food production, which generates about $100 billion a year. More than 247,000 farms in the state cover 130.4 million acres (52.77 million ha). Cotton, corn, grain sorghum, and wheat are the biggest crops, but the largest agricultural product is cattle.

3. Biotechnology

This industry generates more than $75 billion a year. There are 4,500 life sciences companies involved in biotechnology, medical manufacturing, and biomedical research statewide.

4. Chemicals

The state produces 14 percent of the nation's chemicals. There is a cluster of 400 chemical plants and refineries along the Texas Gulf Coast that is the largest complex of such businesses in the world.

5. Computers and Communications

Production facilities for businesses such as Apple and IBM account for 730,551 jobs in Texas. The Texas Emerging Technology Fund gives support for new measures and works to recruit talented researchers.

6. Construction

More people have moved into Texas than any other state since 2010, keeping the 539,542 people in Texas who work at building new houses, roads, and buildings for businesses very busy.

7. Energy

Texas refineries churn out more than 4.7 million barrels of oil each day. Natural gas drilling has supported more than 147,000 jobs in the state, and in 2011 renewable energy sources employed nearly 100,000 people. The state is number one in the nation in wind energy capacity.

8. Health care

The biggest employer in the whole state is health care, with 1,280,332 jobs in this sector (14.57 percent of all jobs). Doctors, nurses, healthcare aides, and those working in retirement homes all over Texas care for the second largest population in the country.

9. Tourism

Hotels and restaurants provided 10.34 percent of all jobs in Texas in 2010. The state is a destination for golfers, there are ninety state parks, and professional and major college sports teams are national attractions.

10. Transportation

There are three hundred airports in Texas, more than in any other state, including twenty-seven commercial airports. The port of Houston ranks number two in the country for foreign tonnage and number two in the country for overall tonnage. Three of the top U.S. seaports by cargo volume are in Texas.

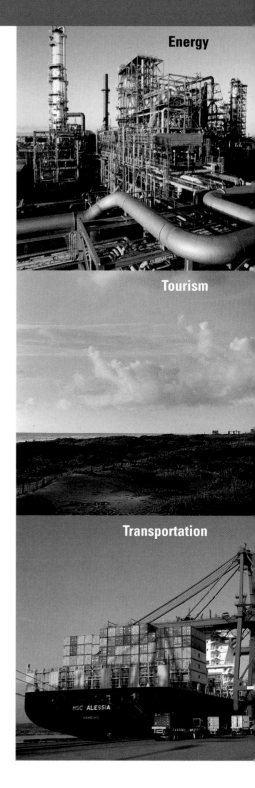

Energy

Tourism

Transportation

Recipe for Beef and Cheese Pinwheels

Beef is the biggest agricultural product in Texas. This recipe celebrates this tasty food, complete with a southwest flair!

What You Need

12 ounces (340 grams) thinly sliced deli roast beef

1 four ounce package (113 g) herb flavored cream cheese

4 ten inch (25.4 cm) flour tortillas

2 cups (473 milliliters) spinach leaves (about 20 leaves)

1 seven ounce jar (198 g) roasted red peppers, rinsed and drained

What to Do

- Spread cheese evenly over one side of each tortilla.

- Place deli roast beef over cheese leaving ½ inch (13 mm) border around edges.

- Place spinach leaves over beef.

- Arrange peppers down the center of the spinach. (Red peppers must be rinsed and dried to prevent soggy tortillas.)

- Roll up tightly and wrap in plastic wrap. Refrigerate at least thirty minutes to overnight before serving. Be sure to wrap tightly to prevent tortilla from drying out.

- To serve, cut each roll crosswise into eight slices. Slice as close to serving time as possible. Arrange cut side up on serving platter.

Agriculture is a crucial part of Texas's economy. Some farmers use crop dusters to spray pesticides to protect their fields.

"integrated circuit." These tiny devices have made the computer and communications revolution possible.

Kilby worked for what was then a medium-sized electronics company called Texas Instruments (TI). Today, TI is a giant in the field, with more than 35,000 employees worldwide. Jack Kilby has been hailed as a pioneer of the high-tech industries. In 1982, he became a member of the National Inventors Hall of Fame. In 2000, he was awarded the Nobel Prize for Physics.

The development of the microchip helped to transform Texas into a center of high-tech commerce. In 2013, Texas was the second-ranked state for number of high-tech jobs and was ranked fourth for adding jobs in technology.

Other Industries

Cotton is still king in Texas, where it is the number one cash crop. One reason that cotton is so profitable is that almost every part of the plant is useful. The fiber becomes cloth, the seeds are used for cottonseed oil, and the husks go into cattle feed.

Not only is cattle ranching a Texas tradition—it is a profitable business. In 2012, income from cattle production was $10.2 billion.

Texas has the largest oil reserves in the nation. Wells in the state produce around one million barrels of oil every day.

Texas is the country's leading producer of wool, which comes from sheep, and mohair, which comes from angora goats.

Texas leads the country in wool production. In 2012, there were 650,000 heads of wool sheep in the state—nearly 100,000 more than second-ranked California.

Transportation is critical in a state with vast areas of sparsely populated land. Texas has a transportation network that accommodates cars, trucks, trains, planes, and ships. More than 71,000 miles (114,000 km) of state roads and 12,000 miles (19,000 km) of railroad tracks thread through the countryside. Trucks can reach 93 percent of the nation's population within 48 hours of leaving the Dallas-Fort Worth Metroplex.

Four deepwater ports on the Gulf Coast handle freighters carrying goods between Texas and foreign markets. There are airports for everything from single-engine crop dusters to international jetliners.

Timber represents more than one-third of total agricultural income in East Texas. Other sections of the state also profit from timber through the manufacture of wood and paper products.

Texas is one of the most visited states in the nation. Texas tourism generates about as much money as the state's agriculture or technology businesses. People come to Texas for many reasons. Some like the excitement of the cities. Others prefer lazing around on Gulf Coast beaches. Families might spend a day or two at the Six Flags Over Texas amusement park near Dallas-Fort Worth or tour NASA's Lyndon B. Johnson Space Center.

The state has something for everyone. Texas is home to ninety mountains that reach altitudes of 1 mile (1.6 km) or more. Ten percent of the state is covered with forests, which includes four national forests and five state forests. Texas also has more than 624 miles (1,000 km) of coastline.

Protecting the Environment

Environmental protection is not limited to parklands and nature preserves. In Texas, taking care of the land is everybody's business. Endangered plants and animals must be protected. Air and water must be kept clean.

Protecting renewable resources is an important part of the state's environmental program. For example, responsible lumber companies in the state plant as many trees as they cut down. This not only protects the forest habitat, it also provides a steady source of timber.

Renewable sources of energy, such as solar and wind power, are also important. Sunlight and wind are limitless and can be used to produce electricity without polluting the air, water, or land. In 1999, the U.S. Congress passed a law requiring power companies to develop these resources. With its wide-open spaces and sunny skies, Texas is perfectly positioned to make the most of solar and wind power. Right now, photovoltaic (solar) systems are powering everything from school crosswalk signs to people's homes.

According to the American Wind Energy Association, Texas in 2013 generated more electricity from wind energy than any other state. With the highest amount of wind capacity installed, Texas produced more than 35.9 megawatt-hours; this is enough power to provide electricity to 3.3 million homes.

The association said the state's main electrical grid, ERCOT, received 9.9 percent of its electricity from wind in 2013. That percentage is well above the national average of 4.1 percent, and it is expected to increase as Texas continues to build more of this green energy capacity.

Major government programs are not the whole story of environmental protection in Texas. Ordinary citizens also get involved. They recycle, volunteer for community cleanup days, and insulate their houses to use less energy.

In the twenty-first century, Texans expect their state to continue to grow and prosper. All the ingredients are in place. Government, business, and ordinary citizens are working together to protect the land. The economy is varied, so that it is not dependent on one or a few industries. Economic forecasts say the economy will grow more than almost every other state. In fact, Texas has been named the top state for businesses by several business magazines. The state's lead in technology will help it make more advances in the future.

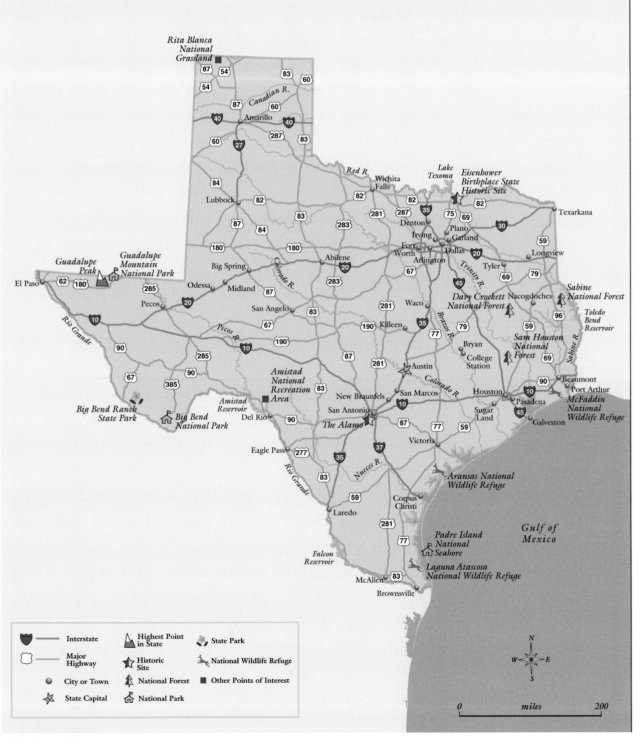

Rita Blanca National Grassland

87 54 83 60
54
87 60 Canadian R.
40 Amarillo 40
60 287 83
60 27
84
Lubbock 82
87 84
180 180
Big Spring Colorado R.
Odessa Midland 87
Pecos 20
San Angelo 83
Pecos R. 67 190
190
285
90
67
90
385

Guadalupe Peak Guadalupe Mountain National Park
El Paso 62 180
Rio Grande 10
90

Big Bend Ranch State Park Amistad Reservoir Del Rio 90
Amistad National Recreation Area 83 New Braunfels
Big Bend National Park San Antonio 87
The Alamo 37
Eagle Pass 277
35
Rio Grande 83 Nueces R.
Falcon Reservoir 59 Corpus Christi
Laredo 281
77
McAllen 83
Brownsville

Red R. Wichita Falls 82
82 281 287 35 75 69 82
Denton
Plano Garland
Irving Dallas 20 59 Longview
Fort Worth Arlington
67 Tyler 69 79
Abilene 283
20 281 Waco Davy Crockett National Forest Nacogdoches Sabine National Forest
283 45 96 Toledo Bend Reservoir
190 Killeen 35 77 79 59
Brazos R. Bryan Sam Houston National Forest 69
College Station 90 Beaumont
281 Austin Colorado R. Houston 10 Port Arthur
San Marcos 10 Pasadena McFaddin National Wildlife Refuge
77 Sugar Land 45
San Antonio 87 77 59 Galveston
Victoria Gulf of Mexico

Lake Texoma Eisenhower Birthplace State Historic Site Texarkana
30

Trinity R.

Aransas National Wildlife Refuge

Padre Island National Seashore Gulf of Mexico
Laguna Atascosa National Wildlife Refuge

Legend:
- Interstate
- Major Highway
- City or Town
- State Capital
- Highest Point in State
- Historic Site
- National Forest
- National Park
- State Park
- National Wildlife Refuge
- Other Points of Interest

N
W   E
S

0   miles   200

TEXAS

MAP SKILLS

1. The highest point in the state is in which national park?

2. What body of water borders southeast Texas?

3. What national wildlife refuge in Texas is the farthest south?

4. Which state highway runs from North Texas through the center of the state?

5. What city is the closest to the Alamo?

6. What river runs through Sugar Land?

7. What Interstate highway would you take to go from Dallas to Austin?

8. State Route 77 connects what three cities?

9. What water feature is just northeast of Denton?

10. What city is closest to the Sabine National Forest?

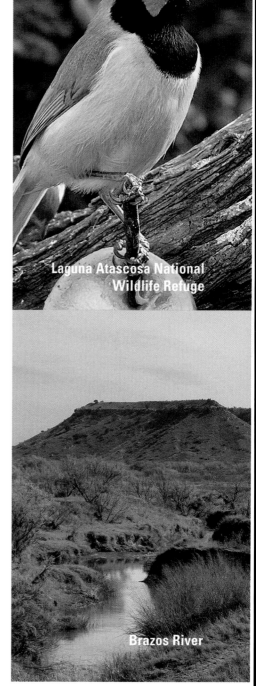

Laguna Atascosa National Wildlife Refuge

Brazos River

1. Guadalupe Mountain National Park
2. Gulf of Mexico
3. Laguna Atascosa National Wildlife Refuge
4. 83
5. San Antonio
6. Brazos River
7. 35
8. Brownsville, Victoria, Waco
9. Lake Texoma
10. Nacogdoches

State Flag, Seal, and Song

The Texas state flag was originally the flag of the Republic of Texas. The blue stripe stands for loyalty, the red stripe for bravery, and the white stripe for purity. It was adopted as the state's official flag when Texas became the twenty-eighth state in 1845. The state flag is called the Lone Star Flag, and that is how Texas got its nickname.

Just ten days after declaring independence from Mexico, the Texas provisional government adopted an official emblem of "a single star of five points, either of gold or silver." Two years later, that star was made the central point of a new state seal, which shows the star encircled by olive and oak branches and topped by the words "The State of Texas."

The state song is "Texas, Our Texas." To read the lyrics or hear the song, visit **www.50states.com/songs/texas.htm#.U6MVT5twq8A**

Glossary

climate	The average weather conditions of a particular place or region over a period of years.
coast	The land along the shore of a lake or an ocean.
commercially	Work that is intended for business or trade.
cowboy	One who tends cattle or horses, especially a mounted cattle-ranch worker.
economy	The way a system of production, trade, and ownership is arranged.
Hispanic	A person living in the U.S. who came from Latin American or whose ancestors came from there.
immigrant	A person who comes to a country to live there.
industry	A group of businesses that provide a particular product or service.
manufacturing	To make into a product suitable for use from raw materials by hand or by machinery.
Native Americans	People who lived on the North American continent before the arrival of Europeans.
oil	A thick liquid is obtained from wells drilled in the ground, and is the source of gasoline, kerosene, fuel oils, and other products.
population	The total number of people living in a country or region.
reservation	An area set aside for use by Native Americans to continue to live by tribal laws and rights as per federal government treaties.
settler	A person who moves into and stays in a new region.
tourism	The practice of traveling for pleasure or the business of encouraging and serving such traveling.

More About Texas

BOOKS

Bredeson, Carmen. *The Spindletop Gusher: The Story of the Texas Oil Boom.* Houston, TX: Bright Sky Press, 2010.

Jerome, Kate Boehm. *Austin and the State of Texas: Cool Stuff Every Kid Should Know* Mount Pleasant, SC: Arcadia Publishing, 2011.

Mountjoy, Shane. *The Alamo: The Battle for Texas.* New York, NY: Chelsea House, 2009.

Rodgers, Kelly. *The Texas Revolution: Fighting for Independence.* Huntington Beach, CA: Teachers Created Materials, 2012.

WEBSITES

The Handbook of Texas Online
www.tshaonline.org/handbook/online

Kids' House (Where Texas Kids Meet Texas State Government)
kids.house.state.tx.us

State of Texas Website
www.texasonline.com

AUTHORS

Linda Jacobs Altman has written many books for young people. She and her husband live in a small California town near a lake, with a house full of pets.

Tea Benduhn writes books and edits a magazine. She lives in the beautiful state of Wisconsin with her husband and two cats.

Hex Kleinmartin, PhD, has taught anthropology, archaeology, and history, and has written several books and papers on these subjects.

Index

Index

Horsham Township Library